A CAREGIVE
PET HOSPICE CARE

For You and
Your Terminally Ill Pet

By
Ruth Gordon

TO THE READER

This handbook is not intended to be read from beginning to end like a story. Scan the Table of Contents and start wherever you have the most immediate need for information. For example, you may wish to start with Deciding if Pet Hospice is Right for You, Pain Control, or When the Time Comes. Then proceed to other topics as your situation changes.

The purpose of this book is to provide general information which can support the role and recommendations of your pet's veterinarian during home hospice care. It is not intended to give advice or make recommendations for any specific animal.

Publishing this book is an investment by the many donors and supporters of Peaceful Passing for Pets, a 501(c)(3) non-profit in Minnesota for the educational benefit of pets and their owners everywhere. To learn more visit www.peacefulpassingforpets.org

ISBN: 978-1-880654-50-7

Author: Ruth Gordon
Design and Layout: Sonya Boushek
Index: Dianna Haught, Words by Haught
Publisher: Alan E. Krysan

Pogo Press
An Imprint of Finney Company
www.finneyco.com

Printed in the United States of America

Table Of Contents

PUBLISHERS NOTE:

The publisher would like to acknowledge and thank the following professionals for taking the time to review, critique, and add input to validate and improve the content provided in this caregiver's guide.

Ann Fischer, DVM
Michael S. Henson, DVM, PHD, DACVIM ONCOLOGY DMV
Rebecca McComas, DVM
The Rev. Mary Piper, Episcopal Priest and Chaplain
Harry Piper, MA , JD
Paula Sallmen, R.N., BAN
Julia Wilson, DVM

This list is likely not inclusive as others have offered advice and guidance throughout the process, for those not listed we apologize for the omission. Without the support of our Board, Donors, Volunteers, and Pet Lovers everywhere this project would not have been possible. Thank you.

Please visit www.peacefulpassingforpets.org for other useful tools including Greif Support; Resources for Pet Owners; Resources for Professionals; FAQ; Ways for You to Help; and much more.

Introduction

This book is written for pet owners who want to care for their terminally ill pet at home, but are just not sure how to do it. For those of you who wish to give that care, this is a resource that should be used while your pet is under the supervision of a veterinarian.

Traditional veterinary medicine generally offers diagnostic testing, treatment of disease, and management of terminally ill pets with medication for symptom control. Then, when a pet's condition declines, owners do their best, play it by ear, and finally take their beloved pet to their veterinarian to be euthanized. Many owners are uncomfortable with this conventional approach. They sense that more could have been done, both for themselves and their pet. In addition, knowing that their pet spent its final conscious moments away from home, perhaps in a place that had been feared, adds to their grief and sense of helplessness. Finally, the experience is even more overwhelming when the owner must leave the veterinarian's office with a leash attached to an empty collar.

There is a better way, both for the owner and for the pet. That better way is pet home hospice. The goal is to maximize both the quality of the pet's final days and its death. It is also an alternative to premature euthanasia. Hospice services make available the guidance of an experienced team of professionals who tailor their recommendations to the needs of each pet and each owner's family. A pet hospice team usually includes a veterinarian, a veterinary technician, a care coordinator, a social worker, a chaplain, and others as needed. At first, the team may be one person, the veterinarian, but it then expands to others as needs increase. The hospice team of professionals can help clients turn a difficult situation into a rewarding time while the family cares for their pet at home. Death may occur naturally, or if euthanasia is required, it can be done at home. After the death, support and grief counseling complete the services of pet home hospice care.

Paula Sallmen, a hospice and oncology nurse and dog lover, worked with terminally ill patients for many years. When she visited homes, she frequently witnessed the family pet staying at the side of the dying person. In one case, the dog had been taught never to get on a bed. Therefore, this pet stayed close to his dying owner, but on the floor close to his bed. Suddenly one day, the dog jumped on the bed and lay beside his owner. Within a few minutes his owner passed away. It was this experience that made Paula ask the question, "Why not apply the comforting practices we use with terminally ill human beings to our loyal terminally ill pets?"

VI

Paula discovered that others had been asking the same question. Building on available information, techniques, and resources, her research culminated in starting a nonprofit organization to provide pet home hospice care, Peaceful Passing for Pets®. This home hospice service seeks to improve the final days of a pet and to assist and support the grieving family. It is patterned after the extremely successful multidisciplinary home hospice services for humans, but it follows the professional guidelines for veterinary hospice care which is unfamiliar to many people.

Peaceful Passing for Pets® will establish avenues for veterinarians to offer home hospice service through their existing practices and will always work under the direction of the pet's veterinarian. It supports families with the expertise of a pet hospice team while they care for their pet at home as long as needed. The program enables families to give optimum comfort care and symptom relief for their pet, at the same time supporting family members while they navigate this difficult journey.

CHAPTER 1

The Evolution of Hospice Care

THE HISTORY OF HOSPICE FOR HUMANS

Hospice is not a new term, but for centuries the meaning of the word has been changing, or you might say, evolving. In the 11th century, hospice referred to the place where the sick and dying went – more like a hospital as we know it today. However, it also referred to the place where travelers stopped for food and rest – more like a motel as we know it. During the middle of the 20th century, hospice took on today's meaning - the care of the dying.

The first modern hospice, St. Christopher's in London, was founded by Dame Cicely Saunders in 1967. After Dame Saunders experienced several personal tragedies, she realized that the approach to care of the dying desperately needed to change. As a nurse, a social worker and, ultimately a physician, she focused her efforts on comfort measures and the control of pain for her dying patients. In addition, Saunders realized that the family needed to be an essential part of planning the care of their loved one.

1

Her ideas were not readily accepted and spread slowly. In fact, it took almost 19 years for her ideas to be widely adopted. Eventually, the St. Christopher's hospice was the model for hospices developed in the United States and throughout the world. Today, hospice care is available in most European countries, Russia, Australia, many African countries, China, Japan, and elsewhere.

So what is Hospice today? It is defined as a special kind of care for persons with a limited life expectancy (usually less than six months). It is 24-hour care that aims to sustain the highest quality of life for whatever time remains for each individual. The emphasis is CARE, not cure, and COMFORT, not treatment. Care includes the patient, the family, special friends, caregivers, and almost always a spiritual advisor. Comfort emphasizes pain control. Because hospice care has broad parameters, it requires a team of knowledgeable professionals who can address the physical, emotional, spiritual, and social needs of both the patient and the family. A physician, nurse, pharmacist, chaplain, social worker, nutritionist, and psychologist are the usual professions that are most commonly needed. Bereavement support and counseling are always a part of the mission of hospice and this service may continue for months after the family member dies.

Hospice is a philosophy as well as a type of care. It can take place in a hospital, a nursing home, a free-standing hospice, or in the patient's home.

Palliative care is another term that the reader may encounter. Palliative care came out of the hospice movement. It also focuses on the relief of pain and prevention of suffering, but it requires the interaction with friends and families for a longer period of time. Palliative care may be given to persons with chronic illnesses and even curable diseases that have a long convalescence. Hospice care focuses on comfort care for persons with a limited life expectancy. Palliative care is more likely to be given in an institution, but it may be given at home also. The goals of palliative care are very much the same as hospice care, but the patient populations differ as does the length of time it may require. This distinction is often overlooked in every-day conversation. Lay people as well as professionals regularly talk of palliative care and hospice care in the same breath so the distinction is largely academic.

By 2010, 1.58 million people had used hospice in the United States, about 900,000 each year. The average length of stay was 57 days and the median length of stay was 22 days in 2004. Most health insurance companies now cover hospice care and, in 1982, Medicare approved inclusion of coverage for hospice care. Current usage data are difficult to obtain because many people begin hospice late in the progression of their disease and may use it for as few as four days. Regardless of the length of time, for most people, hospice has become the preferred way of care for end-of-life situations.

VETERINARY HOSPICE FOR PETS

The role of the veterinarian has been moving toward a more holistic approach to care. The concept of a family-centered practice has emerged. In the past, when medical interventions were no longer beneficial, the veterinarian was quick to recommend euthanasia as a way to limit suffering. Today, you can find veterinarians who provide house calls, mobile services, home hospice advice, and home euthanasia.

Today's veterinarian is asked to help distraught clients to choose between continued treatment, hospice, or euthanasia. This has come about as more and more pet owners consider their pets a part of their family. Therefore, it is not surprising that they seek a different, and some say, a better way to care for pets when they become elderly and/or terminally ill.

According to the 2011-2012 National Pet Owners Survey, there are roughly 78 million pet dogs and 86 million pet cats as well as millions of fish, reptile, equine, and other animals that owners call "pets" in the United States. Among the dog and cat owners, over 65 percent consider their pet a family member. This number is as high as 90 percent in some surveys. This data indicates why pet hospice has become such a welcome movement by many pet owners.

The veterinary hospice movement began in the 1980's when several veterinarians explored the idea of a hospice option in their own practices. One of the first was Dr. Eric Clough, a New

4

Hampshire veterinarian whose wife, Jane, was a hospice nurse. The couple presented a paper on their findings and experiences at the 1998 American Veterinary Medical Association (AVMA) convention in Baltimore, Maryland. In 2001, the American Veterinary Medical Association (AVMA) approved pet hospice guidelines which continue to be updated regularly.

Historically, the first group to have organized the pet/animal/veterinary hospice movement is The Nikki Hospice Foundation, founded in 1996 by thanatologist Kathy Marrachino, Ph.D., with the mission of "Promoting the right to make personal choices concerning a terminally ill companion animal, maximizing quality of life and informing the veterinary community and the public about the value of hospice care". Their first veterinary hospice symposium was held in 2008, a second in 2009 and a third in 2012.

Two organizations have formed to get the educational training and materials in place for end-of-life care. The International Association of Animal Hospice and Palliative Care (IAAHPC) was started in 2009 by Amir Shanan, DVM, who recognized a need for an interdisciplinary group that could work together to promote the knowledge of, and provide the guidelines, for companion animal care at the end-of-life. The IAAHPC is creating a series of certification courses for all professionals who would define themselves as pet hospice workers and is working to provide a comprehensive directory of practitioners for pet owners.

In 2014 the Veterinary Society of Hospice and Palliative Care (VSHPC), co-founded by Katherine Goldberg, DVM, and Page Yaxley, DVM, DACVECC, was established "To advance veterinary medical knowledge, professional education, community engagement, and research in hospice and palliative care."

In 2017 Wiley Blackwell published the manual, *Hospice and Palliative Care for Companion Animals, Principles and Practice* by Amir Shanan, Jessica Pierce, and Tamara Shearer.

In 1993 the American Association of Human-Animal Bond Veterinarians (AAH-ABV) was founded to advance the role of the veterinary medical community in nurturing positive human-animal interactions in society. Guy Hancock, DVM, current member and past president, states the similarity of their mission with hospice "is in hospice's respect for the patient's quality of life and the focus on the human-animal bond."

Basically, the focus of pet hospice is to give pets a safe and caring end-of-life experience in their own home. It aims to maximize the quality of life and the quality of the dying process in order to prevent premature euthanasia. Dr. Cheryl Scott was an early pet hospice provider. Dr. Scott's Home VET Hospice evolved from the many requests she had for home euthanasia. She found that families could learn to provide good home care, including subcutaneous fluid therapy, if they had adequate instruction and assistance. With the emphasis on quality of life, euthanasia is only advised when the parameters you have set for your pet's quality of life can no longer be maintained.

Veterinarians who provide hospice care report that requests for hospice care have gone from 10% to 30% in the last ten years. For those who specialize in this care, 50% of their clients request it.

Hospice gives the family valuable time to be together and to prepare for how and where euthanasia will take place if or when it is necessary. Many pets die peacefully at home before any intervention is needed. Families can also use this time to decide what to do with the remains, what kind of memorial they might prefer, and what kind of memorial service they might wish to have. The hospice team will be visiting on a regular basis. Later, they will be available for advice and grief counseling for as long as it may be needed.

Today, hospice is no longer just for humans. It is now available for pets, something many pet owners have long desired.

RESOURCES

www.peacefulpassingforpets.org, Peaceful Passing for Pets, MN
www.iaahpc.org, International Association for Animal Hospice & Palliative Care
www.aahabv.org, American Association of Human-Animal Bond Veterinarians.
www.avma.org, American Veterinary Medical Association.
www.vethospicesociety.org, Veterinary Society for Hospice and Palliative Care

CHAPTER 2

Deciding if Pet Hospice is Right For You

"SUZU"

Brown eyes, 23 pounds, wagging tail, retired "Best in Show" tan and mahogany Shiba Inu. Her name was Suzu.

My husband and I adopted her when she was six years old. For the next three years she went with me Monday through Friday to the Virginia Piper Cancer Institute where I was the Program Director. She provided joy and laughter, support and comfort to both cancer patients and to staff members. She "worked" at the Cancer Pain Clinic greeting each patient as they arrived and escorting them to the exam room and then returning to the waiting area to greet the next patient. Several times, with patient's who arrived crying, she stayed in the exam room and lay beside the patient obviously aware of their suffering.

In her fourth year in our family Suzu was diagnosed with cancer. She had surgery to remove the tumor, recovered and returned to work with me. Fifteen months later another tumor appeared and again she had surgery. The recovery this time was much more difficult and returning to work was not an option.

When a third tumor appeared in seven months we made the decision to not put her through another operation. Our veterinarian agreed. It was an agonizing decision. As one pet owner put it, "Your heart gets all tied up in the decision your head has to make".

We would do anything to keep her alive but, most importantly; we would do anything to keep her from suffering.

We had a good veterinarian who was kind, supportive, and would see us whenever we needed to come into the clinic. It seemed like each day brought more questions and uncertainty as

8

we cared for Suzu during the last weeks of her life. We did our best, but did we do enough? How could we know for sure that she wasn't in pain? How could we make the moral decision to end her life and what do we base it on? What signs, unique to our beloved pet, were we looking for to know if she was suffering?

We wanted to see her through the end of her life with the unconditional love she gave to us and so many others. We stayed with her constantly, moving her gently from place to place, carrying her up and down the stairs, placing her on her favorite spot on the bed. We did our best, but did we do enough?

As a former hospice case manager I was well aware of the "comfort care" for patients and their loved ones that home hospice provides. Hospice includes the multidisciplinary team, a case manager, chaplain and social worker as well as resources to get questions answered and provide ongoing support.

With the confusion, heartache, and uncertainty my husband and I faced it would have been wonderful if there had been pet home hospice available to us during those last weeks and with the grief we experienced after her passing.

If you are one of the pet families who consider your companion animal a family member, then home hospice is likely to have a strong appeal and becomes a natural extension of that relationship. Pet hospice is family-centered, medically supervised, and dedicated to preserving the human-animal bond while maintaining a quality of life for your pet as long as possible.

The first step is to consult your veterinarian; if this has not already been done. When medical interventions are no longer an option, many veterinarians will suggest other measures for maintaining comfort. The veterinarian will discuss the prognosis of your animal, probable life expectancy, the lack of curative options, and the responsibilities of caring for a pet at home if home hospice is chosen. A family's experience with former pets and their perceptions of those experiences affect each individual differently. Therefore, family members need to weigh not only the goals for their particular pet but the physical, emotional, financial, and time resources that will be required of the family.

Exploring the various components of pet hospice can help you choose what is appropriate for your situation. Families need to recognize that caring for a terminally ill pet at home may require attention for many hours a day for one to two months. The age of family members, family activities, family dynamics, the emotional needs of family members, other pets in the family, and the physical requirements of caring for the pet patient are all considerations that will determine if home hospice is feasible. Basically, you have to evaluate both your own needs and available family resources.

Lastly, costs need to be considered and discussed openly beforehand. You will need to know the estimated costs for veterinary services, hospice services, special equipment that might be needed, and any drugs that will be required. Realistically, costs may become a deciding factor.

If you are the designated caregiver, you will be responsible for monitoring the pet's condition to assure comfort and quality of life, administering medications and treatments, keeping records, and learning how to do other procedures. You may need someone to help care for the pet when you are away from home during the day or to help you with certain procedures. You will need to be cognizant of your own strengths and resources, including time, physical ability, emotional strength, amount of available support from others as well as the family's financial capability before the final decision can be made regarding hospice care.

The question then is how does a pet owner find pet hospice service for their terminal pet? The pet home hospice movement is emerging and, in spite of the increasing number of practices throughout the country, most of the public is confused about what they do, how to find them, and how to assess their quality.

Your veterinarian is always your first resource. Ask if he/she provides hospice care or can refer you to someone who does. If your veterinarian does not provide hospice care and is not aware of one in your community, review the resources provided in this book or Google pet home hospice care in your area. Be sure to read the customer satisfaction reviews. Ask questions about what

10

specifically is provided by the hospice service. Review the *Peaceful Passing for Pets* "Scope of Our Offerings" in the appendix of this guidebook to get an idea of some of the services that could be important to you.

In Minnesota, *Peaceful Passing for Pet's* mission is to make home hospice available to all pets and pet families. Therefore, its primary goal is to partner with veterinarians who want to offer home hospice service within their existing practice. *Peaceful Passing for Pets* provides Care Coordinators who work alongside the veterinarians serving as an extension of their services. They report to, and in conjunction with, the veterinarian, develop a Plan of Care specific to your pet's needs.

The Care Coordinator comes to your home, describes the role of hospice and how it works, an overview of services, the roles of the multidisciplinary team members, information and resources available, and reviews and reinforces orders given by the veterinarian. At this time, you and other family members have an opportunity to express concerns and ask questions. Next, family members are given detailed instruction about the recommended components of care--- nutrition, hydration, pain control, bowel and bladder care, supplies required, any complementary therapies that might be helpful, and tools for how to evaluate your pet's quality of life. The emphasis of care will now be on COMFORT and no longer on treatment or cure. Your animals' quality of life will be your guide from now on.

Follow-up visits, telephone consultations, referral to other professionals, and family support will be provided as needed. Other services may be selected depending on the needs of both your pet and family as time goes on.

Family support is a key component of hospice care because the quality of care of the pet is dependent on the family's physical and emotional strengths.

While your pet is under hospice care your family will have to decide on care of the pets remains, burial arrangements and appropriate memorials. Hospice staff will follow and support clients from the initial visit and throughout the pets' dying process and remain available for bereavement support as long as needed.

Taking care of a pet with hospice home care can seem like an overwhelming and even scary commitment. Pet owners need to know that they have a team that listens to and honors the unique needs, concerns, and wishes of the pet family members.

End-of-life care for our pets goes to the heart and spirit of the bond we have with them. We want their last days to be dignified, comfortable, and enjoyed as much as possible.

This guidebook, websites such as *peacefulpassingforpets.org,* and those listed as resources at the end of each chapter, will help to empower you as your pet's loving caregiver. As a pet owner it is essential to <u>be aggressive in being your pets' advocate</u> for what you believe is the best of care for them.

RESOURCES
www.peacefulpassingforpets.org, Peaceful Passing for Pets, MN
www.aspca.org/pet-care/general-pet-care/end-life-care
www.homevets.org, American Association of Housecall Veterinarians.
www.aahabv.org, American Association of Human-Animal Bond Veterinarians.
www.avma.org, American Veterinarian Medical Association.
csu-cvmbs.colostate.edu/vth/diagnostic-and-support/argus/pet-hospice, Colorado State University Veterinary Teaching Hospital
www.catvets.com, American Association of Feline Practitioners.
www.mnpets.com, MN Pets, gentle end of life care at home
www.solaceveterinaryservices.com , MD, Customized In-Home Care for Your Pet

CHAPTER 3

Maintaining Physical and Psychological Support

The information provided in the next three chapters may seem overwhelming to some readers. Please keep in mind that there are resources available to help you in understanding this material including your veterinarian, the staff at Peaceful Passing for Pets and other established pet hospices. Additional resources include the organizations/ websites listed at the end of each chapter. We provide this information in the hope that you will feel empowered as you care for your terminally ill pet.

SLEEP AND REST

The first step toward maintaining comfort is to assure an accessible resting place. This is necessary for both the pet and the caregiver. For the pet, this may be the bed or an adaptation of the bed that the pet has always used. It is important that it not only be firm but that it also has a soft surface, whether it is a warming bed, a wraparound dog bed, a cushion, or an old blanket or quilt. To minimize any clean-up time, try to use a washable top layer that has a water proof layer underneath. If the pet's bed is high or on an elevated surface, a ramp or a low rise set of stairs will be helpful when the pet becomes weaker, or experiences pain when moving.

When a pet is ill, it will move less frequently. This causes pressure on skin tissue that can result in sores which in turn can become infected. Avoiding pressure on tissue is accomplished best by avoiding any hard surfaces on the pet's resting place. If the pet is too weak to move around on its own, then to prevent pressure sores, assure that bedding and fur is kept clean and dry and turn the pet from side to side every few hours.

The place of the sleeping area is also important. It needs to be where family members can easily visit and keep track of the animal, but it should not be in a high traffic zone where activity can interfere with rest. On the other hand, the pet should not feel isolated. Unfortunately, some pets, especially with elimination problems, become isolated, mainly because of odor. The loneliness that comes from isolation certainly reduces quality of life and can also be detrimental to its physical condition.

In addition, caregivers need to consider themselves. Carrying a cat or small dog up and down stairs is one thing, but if the pet is large, having the bed downstairs is usually best because of easier access to the outdoors. A higher bed area may be best if the caregiver has difficulty stooping, bending over, or sitting on the floor for any length of time. Lift carriers, jackets, and harnesses are available to help move larger dogs. This can also be accomplished by passing a large towel or small blanket under the pet's tummy, holding both ends over the back as a sling. However, this is not recommended for some situations because of discomfort and possible injury to the animal. The commercial devices are safer for the pet and they are very important to protect the owner from unnecessary fatigue, strain, or injury.

A good resting place for the pet does not preclude the necessity for the need to get up, move around, take regular walks, and have play time. This is an important part of assuring that your pet has as many familiar activities as possible. In other words, routine activities need to be maintained, even though the length of time for each may become shorter as the animal loses energy.

NUTRITION AND HYDRATION

Your veterinarian will make specific recommendations for providing your pet with nourishment and fluids. These recommendations will be based on the condition that brings your pet to hospice care. Your Care Coordinator will help you to implement those recommendations. The following suggestions may also be helpful.

While a pet's interest in food and water will ultimately diminish, both remain essential to the comfort and general well-being of the animal early in hospice care. Many pets can stay on the diet they are used to but some with certain disease conditions will require special diets. If a pet's diet is changed, it is best to

15

do so gradually whenever possible. By substituting different foods one at a time over several days, you will find that the pet is more accepting. If there is appetite loss, it may be caused by the underlying disease, pain, or side effects of medications. Your veterinarian will advise you differently in each situation. In some cases, medications may be prescribed to improve appetite.

Your veterinarian may recommend unusual additions to your pet's diet, including human foods or cat food for dogs. Because the wrong choice can cause problems, such as diarrhea or malnutrition, please consult with your veterinarian before making diet changes.

Feeding times will change as your pet's condition changes. Feeding twice a day is fairly common. The pet gets used to the routine and you can plan the times according to your schedule. On the other hand, if your pet can only handle small feedings at a time, you and perhaps other family members will need to provide more frequent feeding times.

It is essential that available food and water be fresh at all times. Moist food should not be left out for more than a half hour to prevent the pet from consuming any bacterial growth. Water needs to be replaced daily for the same reason. Food and water bowls need to be rinsed and cleaned daily. Food can be left out throughout the day only if the food can be kept fresh and there is no other pet that might wish to share it. It is important to keep track of what and how much your sick pet eats because appetite is an indicator of its general condition. Larger pets may eat better if the feeding station is elevated because it is more comfortable.

If a pet cannot eat food as usual, it may be necessary to feed the animal with a spoon or plastic syringe (NO NEEDLE of course). Insert only small amounts of food at a time into the side of the mouth in order to prevent choking caused by too much food in the mouth all at once. Warming a pet's food increases the aroma of food and sometimes increases a pet's interest in eating. Baby food, yogurt, small cookies, ice cream, and the pet's favorite treat can be added for the pet's enjoyment with these feeding methods.

Force feeding during hospice care is not recommended. Sometimes subcutaneous fluids are given for comfort reasons. However, as death approaches, your pet will find food and water less interesting. At this time, it is best just to offer food and water, but if your pet refuses them, he may not need them anymore.

BOWEL AND BLADDER PROBLEMS

Diarrhea and bladder incontinence can be embarrassing to the pet and is certainly challenging to the caregiver. First, the veterinarian needs to seek the cause of these problems. In many cases, incontinence can be treated to improve comfort. However, sometimes these problems cannot be treated and will be on-going.

In this case, the family needs to cope with the incontinence. Letting a dog out more frequently and taking a cat to its box extra times may avert some accidents, but accidents will happen. It is important to maintain hydration to avoid concentrated urine. Therefore, the pet needs plenty of fresh water. Some owners cut back on fluids, trying to minimize accidents, but that can only cause additional problems for the pet. Water should not be restricted. Give a dog more frequent opportunities to go outside. If a dog must be left alone for more than about two hours, a dog walker or neighbor should be asked to let the animal out.

Use of pet diapers may be helpful, but they need to be checked frequently so that urine or stool soaked diapers do not cause odors or skin breakdown. It may help to clip the pet's underside hair if it is especially long. The pet should be cleansed with a waterless or gentle pet shampoo and water (and dried as well as possible) after each change. A hair dryer with low heat and low fan settings can be used for drying. Pet stores usually carry indoor grass-like material or pads in flat containers for dogs that cannot go far to urinate. Some of these aids are disposable and some are washable for re-use.

Long term use of these aids and continued incontinence or diarrhea is a stressful factor for caregivers in home hospice. Caregivers tend to criticize themselves if one or both of these problems result in considering a shorter hospice time. However, the pet may not like the situation either. A cat learned to use its box, and a dog learned to go outside. While they may be

18

embarrassed, they certainly know they are doing something that used to be wrong. If the pets' disease is progressing at the same time, untreatable incontinence and/or diarrhea may or may not become one of the factors in deciding to terminate hospice care and proceed with euthanasia.

RESOURCES

www.peacefulpassingforpets.org, Peaceful Passing for Pets, MN
Local pet stores should carry most of the equipment described.
www.mnpets.com pertinent blogs on many of these topics.
www.pets.webmd.com/dogs/guide/diet-nutrition
(If you have a cat, substitute the word cats for dogs when
        using this website).
www.helpemup.com/ Help 'Em Up Dog Harness

Pain Control

"PEPPER"

There is so much happening in this world yet my attention is on Pepper, my ailing cat. She is 13 years old and very ill.

I give her the medications she needs. She doesn't particularly like taking them. I clean up after her as she has difficulty making it to the litter box. I bring her favorite toy and she seems to perk up but that is only momentarily. Cats can't tell you what is going on. She doesn't complain. I do my best and watch her closely and want to determine if she is uncomfortable or hurting and needs some help. I don't want her to suffer.

My veterinarian referred me to pet hospice. I have received genuine caring and important guidance from them. They have given me information on how to determine Pepper's quality of life. They are there for me when I have questions and their team has provided me with much needed emotional support along the way.

My heart is heavy as I watch Pepper. I spend as much time as I can with her and hold her close. There are those who ask "why put so much effort into her, she is just a cat?" I know they don't understand. I gravitate to those who do understand because they have loved and have known the love of a pet.

Yes, Pepper is a cat but she is also my companion and my friend who has provided me joy and comfort and unconditional love day after day, year after year for over 13 years. Her life on earth seems brief yet I know I will always have her paw print on my heart.

How could I do so much for her? How could I not?

Because the goal of hospice is to provide quality of life, pain control is one of its most important tools. It is also an emotional issue for pet parents because it is so distressing to see their animal suffer. In addition, research supports the importance of addressing the issue of pain. Studies show that pain relief not only aids in comfort but it also lowers the body's stress level and increases the ability to heal.

DETECTING PAIN

First of all, as a caregiver, you need to know that it is often very difficult to tell if a dog or cat is having pain. Therefore, you must be watchful for subtle changes in behavior and activity that may indicate that your pet is having pain. Because pet animals are usually stoics when it comes to pain, a caregiver can be easily fooled. It is thought that pets hide pain because of an instinctual remnant from living in the wild where a weakened animal is vulnerable to attack.

Because pain control is so important to improving your pet's quality of life, your observations are vital. It is easy to suspect pain when an animal is having trouble moving and getting around, but it is more difficult to suspect pain in other pet behaviors, especially in cats. Both cats and dogs potentially may have symptoms such as decreased engagement with family, decreased appetite, decreased activity, or becoming more grumpy or aggressive. Cats may miss the litter box, decrease the amount of grooming or over-groom a specific area, hold the tail down, or rest on its breast bone with the feet tucked under. Dogs may pant or drool, decrease tail wagging, or have difficulty defecating or urinating. Your veterinarian will be able to assess your pet's pain level in a detailed physical examination and then offer recommendations for pain control, but he or she can be helped greatly by your daily observations. As you continue to care for your pet, you will likely begin to notice the relationship of the degree of pain as it relates to subtle behavior changes. See Resources at the end of this chapter for further assistance.

There are many different ways to help control pain for your cat and dog family members. Multi-modal therapy consisting of more than one type of pain control is often best for good results in controlling pain. Oral medications, massage, stretching, chiropractic treatment, laser therapy, and acupuncture are therapies that may work together well to control pain and improve quality of life. Your veterinarian will help you to decide what is best for your particular pet.

ORAL MEDICATIONS

Screening liver and kidney function through blood studies may be recommended prior to placing your pet on a long-term oral pain medication. Different forms of medications can be specifically formulated for pets. Oral medications can be compounded into flavored liquids or treats to help with both the administration and the acceptance of an oral medication.

The veterinarian needs to monitor the drugs as the pet's condition changes. Pets should never be given human drugs unless specifically ordered by the veterinarian.

23

When your veterinarian prescribes a drug or drugs, it is important for you, the caregiver, to keep a daily record of:

1) The pet's behavior before receiving the drug,

2) The time and date the drug is given,

3) The pet's behavior after the drug has taken effect,

4) The time that the effectiveness of the drug seems to taper off.

Effectiveness of pain control and changes in prescriptions for pain control are guided by your observations so good record keeping is essential for the veterinarian to maintain your animal's comfort. All records need to include the date and time of every observation and procedure. Suggestions for ways to administer medications to a cat or dog are discussed in Chapter 5.

Sometimes the veterinarian may ask you to count your pet's pulse beats and number of respirations during a minute. This must be recorded, along with the time, several times a day. Because respirations are visible, they are easy to count. Simply count the number of breaths per minute and record that number with the time and date.

Counting the pulse rate is a little more difficult. For a cat, hold the cat with one hand, cupping the first few ribs. When you feel the pulse, count for ten seconds and multiply that number by 6. The normal cat heart rate ranges from 140 to 200, at the lower end when they are calm. For a dog, find the pulse beat in the lower left front aspect of the chest just behind the elbow. The heart rate for dogs at rest ranges from about 90 to 120 beats per minute, at the lower end for large dogs and at the higher end for small dogs.

Again, count for 10 seconds and multiply by 6. Your veterinarian or care coordinator can help you with these procedures if you are having any problems. Remember, always include the date and time when you record your findings.

ACUPUNCTURE

Veterinarians started using acupuncture in the United States in the 1970's and it has been used to treat many animal illnesses. Acupuncture is the practice of inserting very thin needles into specific points on the body to elicit a biologic response. The stimulation of nerves at these sites has been found to have a profound effect on the entire body including, but not limited to, increased circulation and organ function, pain control, muscle relaxation, and normalized immune function.

Needling trigger points, tight knots within muscle tissue, can help to restore normal function in those muscles, improve range of motion, and decrease pain. It is not recommended to perform acupunctures near skin tumors, but it can still be used in these patients or those with other forms of cancer to help with overall pain control and well-being.

The main risk with acupuncture is injury from improper needle placement. It is important to know that human acupuncturists cannot legally do acupuncture on animals. Therefore, it is highly recommended that you work with a veterinarian certified in acupuncture who understands canine and feline anatomy in order for treatments to be safe and to prevent injury. Treatments are usually on a weekly basis. However, the effects of acupuncture are cumulative so treatments can usually be tapered to a frequency that continues to control pain symptoms. Most dogs and cats will respond to acupuncture after one to three treatments, but this varies from one animal to another.

CHIROPRACTIC TREATMENT

Chiropractic treatment of pets may be given by a veterinarian who has learned animal chiropractic techniques or a chiropractor who has learned animal chiropractic techniques. In Minnesota, animal chiropractors must always have a referral from a veterinarian. If a chiropractor has CVSMT after his or her name, it stands for Certified Veterinary Spinal Manipulative Therapist. Laws in states vary greatly so the reader will have to inquire if animal chiropractic treatments are allowed in your state.

Practitioners must complete at least 210 hours of instruction from one of three programs in the United States that are approved by the American Veterinary Chiropractic Association (AVCA) and then practitioners must be certified by one of three approved certifying organizations.

Animal chiropractic treatment primarily focuses on the relationship between the structure and alignment of the spine as it relates to preserving the health of the nervous system going to various organs of the body. It is most commonly used to treat neuromuscular problems. The purpose of manipulation (or adjustment) of the spine is to restore joint mobility which may relieve inflammation and pain, muscle tightness in an affected part, or improve ambulation.

26

LASER THERAPY

Many veterinarians are using laser therapy as an instrument to reduce pain and inflammation and to promote healing. Laser therapy uses a beam of light at a certain frequency to penetrate the tissue, increasing blood flow and circulation. It affects the tissues on a cellular level stimulating energy production in the cells.

The laser therapy experience is usually comforting and enjoyable for your pet. No sedation or restraint is required. Laser therapy treatments will vary in length and frequency, depending on the condition of your pet. Improvements are often seen after the first visit, but most patients require more than one treatment for optimal benefits. Your veterinarian will recommend a treatment plan specific to your pet.

OTHER THERAPIES

Just as complementary therapies are widely integrated into treatment plans for human health care they are becoming a significant part of pet hospice and palliative care. The popularity of these modalities often stem from the pet owner's desire for less invasive treatments and desire to provide additional ways to support their pet. Often pet caregivers have had success with forms of complementary therapies in their own lives and want the same for their pet.

Some of these modalities include herbal medicines, homeopathy, supplements and essential oils.

It is important that appropriate veterinary care ensures that the measures taken are safe and support quality of life specific to your pet's needs to control pain and other distressing symptoms.

MASSAGE

Massage is a popular form of healing that is gaining popularity today due to our understanding of its benefits through scientific research. Similar to acupuncture, soft tissue massage therapy has been shown to improve digestion, sleep, and immune function, as well as offer pain relief. Moderate pressure massage will stimulate the immune system and decrease stress hormones in the body. Because our bodies have excess stress hormones when ill, decreasing stress through massage can have an overall positive effect on well-being. Massage can also help to increase blood flow to tight muscles and help with both range of motion and mobility.

Many families caring for a dog or cat in hospice will find that simply stroking the animal may become a very important element of care. This may just be a matter of petting the animal in places it has always enjoyed. When family members comfort their pet this way, whether they learn simple massage techniques or not, it reduces their sense of helplessness. In addition, it deepens the connection between the two at this critical time. It needs to be noted that sometimes pets nearing the end of life no longer enjoy touch and may even find it uncomfortable.

Pain Control

There are certified canine and feline massage therapists who know how to perform massage treatments properly that can be beneficial for your pet. You can also learn to perform massage treatments on your pet, but it is very important to have a skilled pet massage therapist or veterinary caregiver with extra training in massage teach you how to safely perform a massage treatment. This is important because improper massage and deep massage techniques can cause pain instead of alleviating it. Therefore, learning proper techniques will spare both you and your pet any unfortunate outcomes.

RESOURCES

www.peacefulpassingforpets.org Peaceful Passing for Pets, MN
www.argusinstitute.colostate.edu, Colorado State University
Veterinary Teaching Hospital
www.allfelinehospital.com/pilling-your-cat.pml
www.aava.org, American Academy of Veterinary Acupuncture
www.ivas.org, International Veterinary Acupuncture Society
www.nbcaam.org, National Board of Certification for Animal
        Acupressure & Massage

Many Colleges of Veterinary Medicine offer services such as acupuncture, chiropractic, and massage. Check with your local schools and universities.

Giving Medications

Before describing procedures, both a caution and a few general comments may be helpful. The caution is that caregivers should NEVER take it upon themselves to give any drug that is not prescribed by the veterinarian because of the possibility of drug interactions, overdose, and/or harm to an animal's particular condition.

As a caregiver, you may be required to do some things that will sound daunting at first, but you will not be asked to do anything that cannot be learned comfortably after one or two demonstrations. While a procedure itself may be easy, most pet owners know that carrying out some of these tasks is not easy, especially with cats. A good sense of humor is useful. A sick, quick cat can often out-maneuver a smart, healthy, quick owner.

And cats of course are experts at hiding. Even with dogs, it may be helpful to say to oneself, "When it comes to medications, especially by mouth, Fido can be a bit ingenious. So, I need to plan ahead and take certain precautions."

Always prepare a medication out of sight of the intended recipient. For drops or an ointment, remove the top so that is ready for quick delivery. Cover a pill, capsule, or tablet with butter or margarine or put it inside a little food such as cheese, a hot dog or canned dog food. If a pill has an odor, it helps to disguise it with a food that smells more strongly so it is less likely to be detected. The slipperiness of butter and margarine is effective for quicker swallowing. There are also some commercially available aids such as a flavored Pill Pocket for dogs and cats. Your local pet store can tell you which ones pet owners prefer.

When giving a medication, be sure to bring along one or two favorite treats. It is important that your pet see the treat when you are about to give a medication.

You know your pet so always have a second person with you if some restraint might be helpful or necessary. You may also need to mummy the animal by wrapping a towel around the body to secure all four legs.

ADMINISTERING PILLS

1) This process is much easier if it is done quickly on the first or second try. To maximize the chance of success, it helps to prevent your dog from easily backing away from you. You can get help from a friend or move your dog to a comfortable place where they cannot easily back up, such as sitting in a corner.

2) Hold the medication between the thumb and forefinger of your dominant hand.

3) If your dog has a short nose, see the instructions for a cat. If your dog has a long nose, place the palm of your non-dominant hand on the top of your dog's nose with your index finger and thumb wrapped behind the large canine teeth (fangs). By doing so, you are gently controlling the entire upper jaw (muzzle) in your hand.

4) Tip your dog's head upward toward the ceiling. It is easier to open the mouth with the head tilted back. Many dogs will open their mouth a bit when you do this, making the process easier.

5) Holding the pill between your thumb and forefinger of your dominant hand, use the next two fingers to open the mouth by pushing down on the front teeth of the lower jaw.

6) Push the pill over the base of the tongue.

7) Close the mouth and hold it closed until your dog swallows. Give verbal praise ("good dog").

8) Blowing a sharp puff of air into your dog's nose right after placing the pill may encourage swallowing.

9) Give a treat, but look around the area to be sure there is no pill lying about!

10) It is always best if a dog drinks a little after a pill. Offer fresh water or broth or you can use a syringe (no needle) to encourage intake. If the medication can be given with food, a small meal can be used instead of water.

ADMINISTERING LIQUID MEDICATIONS

1) As with administering pills, it is helpful to prevent the dog from backing up. Get help from a friend or have the dog sit in a corner.

2) Control the head and tilt backward. This can be done by holding the entire upper jaw as you would for administering pills, leaving the lower jaw to move freely. Another option is to loosely close the jaw and tilt the head up with your non-dominant hand cupping the dog's cheek, thumb wrapped under the lower jaw bone and fingers wrapped over the top of the nose (muzzle).

3) Holding the syringe (no needle) in your dominant hand, place the tip just inside the cheek near where the upper and lower lips meet.

4) Slowly dispense the liquid. The dog will swallow automatically.

5) If a large amount of fluid needs to be given, be sure to pause regularly to allow time for the dog to swallow before more fluid is dispensed.

GIVING MEDICATIONS BY MOUTH TO CATS

1) Most cats first need to be wrapped (mummied) in a bath towel so that the front and back paws are secured downward. A restraint bag may be found at pet stores. A second person is highly recommended.

2) Place the palm of your non-dominant hand over the cat's forehead with your thumb on one side of the cheek (upper jaw behind the fang) and your index and middle fingers on the other cheek. If your hands are large enough, wrap your smallest fingers behind the ear so that you are holding the entire top of the cat's head gently but firmly and comfortably in one hand.

3) Tilt the head back.

4) Holding the pill between the thumb and index finger of your dominant hand, use your other fingers to press on the lower jaw to open the mouth.

5) Push the pill on the back of the tongue.

6) Close the mouth quickly and hold it shut until your cat swallows. A sharp puff of air in the nose may prompt swallowing.

7) It is always best if a cat drinks a little after a pill. Offer fresh water or broth or you can use a syringe (no needle) to encourage intake. If the medication can be given with food, a small meal can be used instead of water to assure the pill passes to the stomach and does not cause irritation in the food passageway (esophagus).

8) Look around to assure that the pill has not been expelled.

Alternate Method: *If the veterinarian allows you to crush the pill, try putting it in cream cheese. The cat may lick it off your finger or off its own paw.*

NOTE: *When giving liquids to a cat, use a plastic bottle, eye dropper, or syringe without a needle.*

---

1) Bundle the cat as described above.

2) Fill applicator with not more than 3 teaspoons of liquid or as directed.

3) Tilt the chin upward and dispense the liquid into the cheek pouch SLOWLY, giving time for the cat to swallow a little bit at a time.

GIVING EYE MEDICATIONS TO A CAT OR A DOG

How to administer eye medications depends on the breed and species. For many dogs with loose skin, the lower eyelid technique works well. However, for many dog breeds and cats, it is easier to pull the upper lid back to expose the globe for the drop. Whatever works is best. Most animals will not sit still for eye drops, at least not after the first one, so some gentle restraint is necessary for success. Have a second person hold the animal if you need help.

1) Assemble your supplies (moistened cotton balls, eye medications).

2) To prevent your pet from backing away, get help from a friend or have them sit in a corner. For cats and small dogs, some find it helpful to kneel with the pet between your legs. Many cats do best using the "mummy" towel wrap (see giving pills by mouth).

3) Clean any discharge from the eye with a damp cotton ball.

4) Restrain the head and tilt it upward using the technique most comfortable for you. For most people, this involves restraining the head with one hand wrapped around the muzzle (see giving liquid medications by mouth) while administering the eye drops with the other.

5) Holding the medication between the thumb and index finger of your dominant hand, brace the base of your hand against the face and pull downward on the lower lid (or upward on the upper lid) to open the eyelids.

6) Being careful not to touch the eye, squeeze a drop of medication into the lower lid or onto the white of the eye near the upper lid.

7) Let your pet blink, but do not allow rubbing.

8) For ointments, squeeze out a 1/4 inch strip of ointment and lay the strip along the inner edge of the opened eyelid.

9) Give a treat!

GIVING EAR MEDICATIONS TO A CAT OR A DOG
– Have a second person hold the animal if you need help

1) Hold the outside ear flap out and back with your non-dominant hand.

2) Have the medication ready in your dominant hand and squeeze the prescribed ointment or number of drops into the ear canal (the opening going inside the head).

3) Gently massage the side of the ear. Your pet will shake its head.

4) Give a treat.

GIVING SKIN MEDICATIONS TO A CAT OR DOG

When a lotion or ointment is prescribed by your veterinarian, he or she may clip the fur over the lesion. After a brief demonstration, you will learn to cleanse the area with clear water or a prescribed cleanser. Either pat the area dry or dry with a cool hair dryer on low speed. Then apply the medication. It is important that skin lesions be protected from licking and/or scratching to prevent infection and allow healing. Many families prefer to avoid Elizabethan (lampshade) collars if possible, but they are necessary in some cases. If a T-shirt or sock are used to cover a lesion, extra care should be taken to keep the area clean and dry, checking the wound at least twice daily and changing the cover when soiled.

GIVING INJECTIONS

Caregivers will seldom be asked to give injections. A veterinarian will nearly always give any intravenous injections and any one-time intramuscular injection if there is any chance of an allergic reaction. However, you may need to learn how to give intramuscular injections or subcutaneous injections if the pet has diabetes or needs hydration. Your veterinarian will provide instructions for one of two ways, subcutaneous (under the skin) or intramuscular (into a muscle).

1) Have a second person restrain the pet if needed. While the procedure is not very painful, there is enough discomfort that this may be necessary.

2) Draw the medicine into a sterile syringe.

3) If there are any air bubbles in the syringe, point it upward, flick the syringe with a finger and press the plunger until the bubbles are gone.

4) Part the hair at the site of the injection and cleanse it according to your veterinarian's instructions.

5) Insert the medication as instructed, remove the needle and syringe, and gently press the site for a few seconds.

6) Give a treat.

RESOURCES

www.peacefulpassingforpets.org, Peaceful Passing for Pets, MN
www.pets.webmd.com/dogs (if you have a cat, substitute cats for dogs
    in this website)
www.vetmed.wsu.edu, (search cat or dog medications)

*Acute pain scales are located in the appendix.

When the Time Comes and Quality of Life

IF IT SHOULD BE

If it should be that I grow weak,
And pain should keep me from my sleep,
Then you must do what must be done,
For this last battle can't be won.

You will be sad - I understand.
Don't let your grief then stay your hand,
For this day more than all the rest,
Your love for me must stand the test.

We've had so many happy years.
What is to come can hold no fears.
You'd not want me to suffer so -
The time has come. Please let me go.

I know in time that you will see
The kindness that you do for me.
Although my tail its last has waved,
From pain and anguish I've been saved.

Please do not grieve -- it must be you
Who has this painful thing to do.
We've been so close, we two, these years,
Don't let your heart hold back its tears.
– Author Unknown

Hospice care provides a special time for you and your family to be with your pet. It also has the advantage of giving you, the caregiver, time to prepare both psychologically and practically for your pet's death. It gives you the opportunity to learn about your options related to preparation for your pet's death, care of its body after death, and selection of memorials that are appropriate for you and your family.

Euthanasia is the Greek word for "good death." It is emotionally very difficult to think about making plans for your pet, both before and after death, whether it is a natural death or by euthanasia. Because anticipatory grief (that grief one feels before a pet dies) is so painful, it often prevents some of us from making such plans. First of all, many of us hope that natural death will come before we need to decide on euthanasia. Realistically, however, this does not always happen.

Dr. Michael Henson, Associate Professor at the University of Minnesota College of Veterinary Medicine and the Section Chief, Oncology states, "Almost every day, pet parents tell me they want to say goodbye before there is significant suffering. Almost all are interested in palliative care, some interested in hospice, but yet they want to euthanize when it is the right time. Almost all pet parents do not want medications that change alertness and attitude. They would rather say goodbye than have sufficient pain medications such that the patient is somnolent. It depends on the disease, but natural death without significant opioids is often not without suffering, so euthanasia is the greatest gift."

No matter how stressful it is to decide a time for euthanasia, you may ultimately find that to end your pet's suffering is indeed a gift and an act of love and compassion.

DECIDING THE TIME

Caregivers usually ask, "How will I know when the time comes?" Some will say, "Your pet will tell you." Not in words, of course, but they do "tell" us a lot in their own ways. As you care for your pet, you will learn more and more about what continues to make your dog or cat happy and comfortable, so in this sense, your pet does tell you. You, the caregiver, will begin to set new and different parameters for what is an acceptable quality of life for your particular situation. You will ultimately become your pet's advocate for defining its quality of life or the lack of it.

User-friendly Quality-of-Life (QOL) assessment scales are available to help veterinarians and pet owners make proper assessments and decisions at the end of a life. It is generally agreed that the pet's owner is best qualified to evaluate QOL but a team approach is important to provide empathetic support when end-of-life decisions are made.

Dr. Alice Villalobos, director of Animal Oncology and Consultation Service, Woodland Hills, California and Pawspice, Hermosa Beach, California states, "It is up to the veterinary professionals and to the pet's individual caretaker to design an end-of-life program. The program needs to address each factor that deals with quality of life openly and honestly." We can be very proactive in helping pets achieve an improved score on their evaluations." To accomplish this she has created a Quality of Life Scale "to provide an easy guideline for assessment of the pet so that family members can maintain a rewarding relationship and nurture the human-animal bond. This Quality of Life scale offers some objectivity while remaining sensitive to the caregiver's wishes. It will relieve guilt feelings and engender the support of the veterinary team to actively help in the care and decision-making for end-of-life care."

JOURNEYS: A Quality of Life Scale for Pets has been developed by Katie Hilst, DVM after hundreds of conversations over the years with pet owners and their families making the decision to euthanize their pet. Dr. Hilst states, "Sometimes, after the discussion, people realize that their pet is enjoying life, and they still have time left with their pet. Other times, people realize their pets are suffering more than they were aware, so they choose the final act of caring. In either case, the JOURNEYS scale is meant to get pet owners thinking and considering the factors that affect your pet's happiness and sense of well-being. This tool, to be used as a starting place to explore your pet's quality of life, and address your concerns with your veterinarian, is included in the appendix of this guide.

This may sound a bit too abstract, so learning how other pet owners have made their decisions may be helpful. You will notice a wide range of circumstances that cause people to decide "when the time came." In his book, *Dog Years: A Memoir*, Mark Doty describes one morning finding his old dog, Arden, crying out in the kitchen as he lay in a pool of urine and feces. Over the past few years, he and his partner had used acupuncture, herbs, special diets, and various pain drugs to keep him comfortable, but on that morning they cleaned Arden and called their veterinarian to end Arden's suffering.

In the book, *A Dog Year,* Jon Katz watched his dog, Julius, "lose steam." He lagged behind in walks; he lost interest in sniffing the wonders of outdoors, and he became more and more lifeless. With the diagnosis of colon cancer and no possibility of further treatment, Katz finally chose a day to visit his veterinarian. Jon held Julius and stroked him lovingly as the drugs of euthanasia took over.

My golden retriever, Ben, had lymphoma and lost his sense of fun very rapidly. One night he could not get up on our bed as usual, so my husband picked him up and laid him on the bed. Ben cried out in pain as he was moved. The next morning Ben went out in the yard as usual. When he came in the house, he could not stop shivering and shaking. He sat down beside me, gave me a very quick glance and then looked forward into space. He did not come for a scratch as usual and I read his glance as, "Please help me". We made our appointment with our veterinarian that afternoon.

The singer, Fiona Apple, canceled a South America concert tour in 2012 to be with her dying dog. For canine or feline family members, it is vital to stay with them during their last days so you can assure yourself that natural death or euthanasia prevents any undue suffering. In other words, Fiona Apple wanted to be the one to decide when her pet's quality of life crossed from acceptable to unacceptable using her criteria. She exemplifies the need for the owner who knows the pet best to be there to make such an important decision.

When it is time for you to make this difficult decision, try not to back away emotionally as the end comes. Sometimes the fear of a painful or distressing death becomes overwhelming and distorts our ability to see a situation clearly. In this case, we may unconsciously ignore important symptoms.

Throughout the years that you and your pet have lived together, you have learned the meaning of many non-verbal communications between the two of you. Now is the time to become especially sensitive to changes in your animal, both behavioral and physical. To aid in your decision making, Dr. Julie Reck, DVM, suggests asking some of the following questions in her book, *Facing Farewell: Making the Decision to Euthanize Your Pet:*

- Can your pet get up and down without assistance?
- Does your pet have frequent urine or bowel accidents in the house?
- Does your pet still enjoy toys?
- Does your pet still enjoy going outdoors?
- Has your pet lost vision and/or hearing?
- Does your pet spend more time alone, hiding, or in seclusion?
- How is your pet's appetite?
- Does your pet have more bad days than good days?

Keeping a daily record of the answers to these questions will help you to answer, "Am I maintaining my pet's quality of life or am I prolonging the suffering?" It is often very hard to let go because of your own emotional pain, usually in the form of "anticipatory grief" which may include dread, anger, anxiety, and even physical symptoms. However, when your pet can no longer live with dignity and be pain-free, it is probably time to make your decision. When it seems close to the end, it is usually best to proceed a day too early as opposed to a day too late because terminal changes proceed quite rapidly.

This is the time you will need to call on your support group. Be kind to yourself. Spend a quiet time with your pet, telling him/her how much he/she has meant to your life and that he/she will never be forgotten. Speak to your pet, communicating as a 2-way team – listen and talk. Use a soothing voice so that your anxiety is not communicated. Like all grief, your experience will differ from others so do not compare your reactions to those of others.

THE QUESTION OF GUILT

As an Episcopalian chaplain and priest, a lover of pets and co-founder of a pet loss support program in Montana, Reverend Mary Piper has walked closely with many individuals grieving the loss of a beloved pet. She notes that in her experience, people often refer to "guilt" either in anticipating, or having made, the decision for veterinarian-assisted death for their companion animal. Sometimes people wonder, "Did we do this too soon? other times, "Did we wait too long?" The question "How can I play God?" may be experienced in either case.

Rev. Piper shares two examples:

> Clearly distressed, tears in her eyes, Jennifer said, "I still wonder if there was something else I could have done." "Could a different treatment have been tried?" or "Would a different pain medication have given a few more days by providing greater comfort?"

> On the other hand John said, "I regret that I waited too long to accept euthanasia. Now, as I look back, I recognize that my pet was suffering. If I had it to do again I would not wait as long but, in the moment when my heart was hurting, the decision was too hard for me to make."

Both Jennifer and John are expressing a common aspect of grief that confronts us with the limitations of our knowledge (and foresight) as human beings, and the second guessing that often goes along with that, in particular when we feel that the life of a beloved animal is or was in our hands. While the pet owner is generally understood to be responsible for decision-making regarding treatment and end-of-life choices on behalf of their pet, a team approach can provide welcome and empathetic support when such decisions must be made. Hospice is designed to provide support during these challenging times with a multidisciplinary team including chaplains and social workers. The goal is the best quality of life (QOL) for the pet and optimal support for the pet owner, given the emotional and caregiving challenges of the last chapter of a pet's life. User-friendly QOL assessment scales are available to help veterinarians and pet owners, with desired clinical guidance from veterinarians, make the right compassionate and ethical decisions at the end of a life. Utilizing such tools can provide a measure of objectivity in evaluating a pet's quality of life, and can provide information for the veterinary team as they offer guidance regarding an individualized care plan. This assures pet owners maximum support in decision-making on behalf of their beloved pet and offers the best possible assurance that decisions will be made "not too soon," but also "not too late."

In addition to the feelings of guilt mentioned above, other experiences of deep pain are often expressed by those who love a companion animal, such as "Where am I sending them?" "Why does my gentle animal have to suffer?" "Does my pet have a spirit?" "Will I see her again?" The soulsearching and anguish that pet owners experience is real and can cause much suffering. These are spiritual questions. In human hospice team members address the four kinds of suffering : physical, emotional, social and spiritual. The same is true for pet hospice. It is important for pet owners who face end-of-life for a beloved pet to know that they can ask for help from a hospice chaplain and other members of the hospice team.

EUTHANASIA – BEFORE AND AFTER

If euthanasia is to be done at the veterinarian's office, you might ask for a sedative to be given to your pet at home before going to the office to allay any anxiety that it may have. However, most hospice pets are euthanized at home so there is an opportunity to plan the setting. Where do you want your pet to be for the procedure? Do you want it in his or her bed, a special room, or outdoors? Who do you want present? Would you like a memorial paw print made? Would you like candles, special lighting, music, spoken memories, flowers, or prayers?

What can you expect when your pet is euthanized? Most veterinarians use a two-step procedure. First, the animal is sedated, using a needle and syringe near the shoulder or other area where the insertion is out of the pet's peripheral vision. The medication is calming and induces sleep, not too different from anesthesia. After the sedation has taken effect, the euthanasia drug is given into the vein. In 10 to 90 seconds the heart will stop. Your pet will not show any signs of suffering or awareness of the end, but earthly suffering will have ended. After the procedure, the veterinarian will use a stethoscope to be assured that death has occurred. Your pet may pass away with eyes half open. Soon afterwards, the animal may twitch or seem to take a few breaths. This is actually the process of energy leaving the muscles. Finally, urination and defecation may occur after a few minutes.

BURIAL AND MEMORIALS

The first decision is whether to have cremation or not. If the decision is to bury the body, it is essential that you consult your city administrator to find out what laws govern pet burial in your area. Laws vary greatly.

Today, many people choose cremation, and your veterinarian can guide you to a company that provides the services that you desire. You will be asked to request either individual cremation or group cremation where there is co-mingling of ashes with other animals. You may wish to have the crematorium come for the body and return the ashes to you or to your veterinarian's office. Ashes will usually be delivered in an urn or cardboard box containing a sealed plastic bag to avoid any spillage. Or, you may wish to take your pet directly to the crematorium, lay your pet in the retort, and remove the ashes yourself.

Many pet parents wish to have a memorial service similar to what you might have for a family member because your pet was, after all, an important family member. My husband and I chose to have our special service with just the two of us when we buried Ben's ashes under a special red maple tree that we had planted in his memory. You may wish to scatter the granular ashes in one or more special places. You may wish to use a pet cemetery and have a memorial stone. You and or friends may donate to a local animal shelter in your dog or cat's memory. Some families set a memorial table displaying reminders of the pet's life. You may wish to purchase an urn and keep the ashes with you wherever you might live. You may wish to create your own memorial service with readings, prayers, flowers, and invited guests.

51

Many people feel they can't ask a "spiritual authority" to assist with memorial services because they have been told that pets don't merit that, pets don't go to heaven, pets don't have a soul, etc. Pet hospice, with its interdisciplinary team, provides a safe place to request help and receive support and spiritual counseling from a hospice chaplain. Reverend Mary Piper has found that it is often very healing to have a ritual and a public acknowledgment of the pets' life. This has had great meaning within human hospice and is a practice that will be honored within pet hospice.

Each pet is different and each family is different so remember your special friend in whatever way that is right for you and your family.

It is also possible to preserve the body. Rather than taxidermy, a freeze-dry process is used more commonly today. This process was originally developed for preservation of museum specimens.

It is interesting to note that there are also more exotic tributes which might be affordable and appeal to a few. A recent newspaper article was entitled "Pet burials range from bottom of sea to sky above." Instead of cremation, they described Aquamation, a water-based technology that leaves the ashes a powdery white ash. There is a company that takes strands of a pet's hair or ashes and turns them into a diamond ($2,000 to $24,000). In California and Hawaii, services for burial at sea are available and in Florida, a company provides mourners a chance to send ashes-filled balloons that release five miles up.

It is important to remember that a simple, inexpensive tribute to the love and joy your pet brought to you and your family is as sincere an expression of gratitude as more elaborate and expensive expressions. Your pet was grateful for his or her life with you, not for what you do after its death. What you do afterwards is for you and your family.

RESOURCES

www.peacefulpassingforpets.org, Peaceful Passing for Pets, MN

Anderson, Moira. *Coping With Sorrow, on the loss of your pet,*
    2nd ed., Alpine Publications, *Loveland,* CO, 1996.

Kaplan, Laurie, *So Easy to Love, So Hard to Lose; A Bridge to*
    Healing Before and After Loss of a Pet, Jan Gen Press, 2010.

McComas, Rebecca. *Knowing When It's Time to Say Goodbye*,
    www.MNpets.com

Reck, Julie, *Facing Farewell, Making the Decision to Euthanize*
    Your Pet, Dogwise Publishing, 2012.*

csu-cvmbs.colostate.edu (Search: Pet Hospice)

www.sayinggoodbyetoyourangelanimals.com, Pet loss and
    Bereavement

www.iccfa.comnode/2562/AboutPLPA
    (Pet Loss Professionals Alliance)

www.lapoflove.com (Pet Quality of Life Scale and Daily Diary)

www.pet-loss.net, (Pet Loss Support page)

www.petsrememberedcremation.com, (Cremation Services)

www.aplb.org (Association for Pet Loss and Bereavement)

inhomepeteuthanasia.com (In Home Euthanasia National Directory)

www.pawspice.com/q-of-l-care/new-page.html, Quality of Life Scale

*Has helpful questionnaires for decision making

CHAPTER 7

Bereavement

Of life and death and love and dogs

I've lost my best buddy. But even now, perhaps he's showing me the way.

Down in the country, summer has passed its dazzling zenith — if only just.

Amid the farms and bluffs of southeastern Minnesota, where I've long been fortunate enough to squander occasional summer afternoons, the days on one recent late-July weekend still seemed lazy and lingering — but not quite so endless as they had felt only weeks before.

A few of the blazing perennial blossoms had begun to fade and wither. The sea of corn buffeted by the breeze all across the rolling hills — some of it immensely tall now — had lost its deepest jungle green and commenced the turn from growth to ripening.

It might just be me, of course, imposing this patina and pathos on an impassive landscape. I often am what people call "too serious." And lately I have an excuse.

My closest companion, best buddy and spiritual adviser has died. He was a 12-year-old collie mix, a courageous and mischievous goofball named Lucky who taught me the kind of things only the four-legged angels who visit our world can teach.

I recognize the shameless self-indulgence involved in bothering readers with my grief over a lost pet. There's nothing very special, much less newsworthy, about the experience. But maybe that's the point.

Life delivers more fearful and devastating blows than the loss of a beloved animal, but many have shared (or will share) this startlingly bone-deep pain and lonesomeness. By confessing it, maybe I can hope in some small way to help us all comfort one another.

From a commentary by D.J. Tice in the Minneapolis Star Tribune, August 2015 (Full commentary in Appendix)

Grief has many facets. First of all, it is a highly individual experience. It often comes in stages that may include shock, anger, denial, loneliness, self-pity, guilt, regret, and over-all sadness. Some of these feelings may be experienced more intensely than others, but know that your feelings will come and go, eventually with less intensity, and with less frequency. Ultimately, acceptance will come, but reminders of your loss may trigger grief even many years later. In the beginning, when you are feeling most overwhelmed, it is helpful to seek outside help and support.

Many people find that the grief accompanying the loss of a pet is more intense than the grief accompanying the loss of a parent. This of course adds to one's guilt, but there are reasons for this phenomenon. One reason is that there is generally greater understanding and support associated with the loss of a parent.

The same level of support is often lacking when we lose an animal member of the family. In addition, there is less emotional baggage with the loss of a pet. For example, your pet never set boundaries in bringing you up, never argued with you about your activities, or disciplined you when you went astray. In other words, you inevitably had conflicts with your parent no matter how much you loved him or her. Your pet, on the other hand, always greeted you with enthusiasm, accepted you, and loved you unconditionally. Some people say that they learned more about love and the giving of love from their pet than from a parent or any other person.

Because we seem to be a feeling-avoidant society, it is hard to acknowledge that grieving is so painful and that it is such a gradual and often slow process. It can take weeks, months, and sometimes years. It cannot be ignored. In fact, if healing is to take place, it must be expressed through crying, writing, talking, or whatever outlet that an individual finds helpful.

Some people find it is beneficial to write about how they felt about their beloved companion. Artists like to paint or sketch their memories. Others may need to talk about how they feel while still others deal with their feelings in less obvious ways. I wrote a small book, *Magic Dog,* the biography of our golden retriever, Ben. I also spent hours making a scrap book of pictures of all the good times we had. A friend who lost her cat gathered those who knew her pet for a special time to reminisce about their times with her. One person's memory reminded another person's memory of her cat, Julie. At the end of the gathering, Julie's life had actually been eulogized. Donating to an animal organization in the pet's memory can be helpful to families. Whatever ways the pet is remembered and honored serve to comfort and to heal the mourners.

Because everyone grieves differently, some family members will need to talk while others will prefer to reflect and be more private. Many people experience a disruption in their waking, sleeping, and eating routines. Some people may wish to reduce their social activity by staying home and being alone more than usual. Employed people often take days off from work. Almost everyone is upset by those who seem to lack understanding of what you are experiencing. Grief produces not only emotional but also physical symptoms.

You will have friends who have experienced what you are suffering as well as friends who do not understand at all. In the beginning, it is best to stay away from anyone who says, "But it was just a cat (or a dog)," because they can make you feel even more isolated and lonely. Stay with friends who understand your grief and those who let you cry. You may want to join a support group and/or meet with the social worker or chaplain from your hospice organization. There is a lot of help available so be sure to use it.

Take good care of yourself. Because grief depletes you physically as well as emotionally, it can be overwhelming. You are also tired from the weeks of caretaking. Exercise, even if it is an effort to take a walk or bicycle a mile. Eat a healthy diet and try to get proper sleep. Give yourself the gift of private time and social time with understanding friends. The time will come when you will remember the gifts that this pet gave you, and you will be glad for having had this companion in your life.

WHAT TO TELL CHILDREN

What you tell children depends on their age, their experiences with death, your religious beliefs, and individual circumstances. For many children, the death of their pet is their first experience with death. In this case, the parent's explanation will be especially important. Remembering that young children think in more concrete terms than older children, a few recommendations may be helpful.

First, do not try to shield a child from sadness. This is actually impossible since attempts to do so can confuse a child who can usually sense that there is more going on than what is being said.

Second, be honest and use simple terms, such as "He or she won't be back." Remind the child that the beloved pet can always be brought back in memory. You can cry together. This helps the child to understand that grieving is normal for both of you.

Third, do not say "He or she was put to sleep" or "He or she went to sleep." Younger children especially may worry that this may happen to you, the parent, siblings, other pets, or even to himself or herself when they go to sleep at night.

It may be helpful to have the child view the deceased pet's body in order to say "Goodbye." If circumstances allow it, letting a child do this brings reality to the situation. Let the child be present at the euthanasia or participate in the memorial service if that seems appropriate.

Children may express grief in non-verbal ways such as withdrawal, irritation, or loss of appetite. Encourage them to talk about their feelings. Be especially reassuring if the child feels any responsibility for the pet's death. Children may also be candidates for a support group.

Each child may find an individual way to memorialize their special friend. Give them time to draw pictures, select a special picture for framing, or make a clay model of their companion animal who has just died. Help the child to remember what joy he or she gave to the pet when they played together.

WHEN OTHER PETS GRIEVE

One often forgets that other family pets are likely to grieve. Research has demonstrated that animals mourn the loss of their family members. Apes, elephants, dogs, birds and other species have been studied extensively. Cross-species mourning, such as an elephant mourning a dog, is not unusual either. Some animals show an initial reaction by crying, screaming, or other utterances. Some will be quiet at first, but then search for the lost one and become apprehensive later on. Dogs may become depressed, listless, stop eating, or become clingy. Some choose to sleep where their companion slept and some may start to eat out of the companion's bowl. We have all seen a pet mourn the loss of its human friend, but we sometimes forget that a pet can mourn its animal companion also.

The ASPCA Companion Animal Mourning Study found that two-thirds of dogs exhibit behavioral changes when a household companion dog dies. The negative behavior sometimes lasted six months and even up to a year or more in some cases.

Like people, animals grieve differently. It is recommended that other household pets see their friend after death. Some may nudge the animal as if to see whether there is a response. Another may lie down beside the animal while another may just walk away. Afterwards, the behaviors that might arise include loss of appetite, wandering around aimlessly, being clingy, or being less friendly. These changes are usually temporary but occasionally they become permanent.

61

Judith Lewis Mernit reports that after her dog, Seamus, died, her dog Spud was never able to recover from the loss. Spud was given a clean bill of health just days before he died, apparently of a broken heart.

My uncle had a standard poodle, Cocoa, and a beautiful collie, Ronnie, who were inseparable. Before the days of leash laws, they played together in their neighborhood while my uncle was at work. One day Cocoa walked in front of a car and was killed. Ronnie was a witness to the accident. For a week, Ronnie stayed in his back yard, and howled for hours. After expressing his grief, he was gradually able to return to his new life without his best friend.

It is a helpless feeling to watch a pet grieve, but there are a few things you can do to be of help. First of all, give the companion some extra attention. It is also recommended that the grieving pet spend time with toys they played with together. Finally, extra exercise may also help. In extreme cases, an anti-depressant may be indicated. It is also recommended to maintain the same routine as much as possible, eating, walking, and playing at the same times as before the loss.

SUMMARY

Bereavement is a universal experience, but it is experienced differently by each individual. Its pain may be shared or not, but it must be expressed in one or more ways in order to have a resolution. In spite of the pain from losing a pet, most human companions agree that pets are very special family members who deserve to be honored for their lives of devotion, many contributions, fun, and unconditional love. Your pet's legacy will be priceless memories.

RESOURCES

www.peacefulpassingforpets.org, Peaceful Passing for Pets, MN
ASPCA, 1-877-474-3310, American Society for the Prevention of
        Cruelty to Animals Pet Loss Hotline.
Iams Pet Loss Support Hotline, 1-888-332-7738,
King, Barbara J. *How Animals Grieve*, University of Chicago Press, 2013.
Mernit, Judith Lewis. "Seamus and Spud" in Cherished,
        New World Library, Novato, California. 2011.
Pierce, Jessica. The Last Walk, *Reflections on Our Pets at the End of
        Their Lives,* The University of Chicago Press, 2012. aplb.org
(Association of Pet Loss and Bereavement)
www.animalhumanesociety.org/or call 952-HELP-PET (952-435-7738)
www.pet-loss.net Ten tips for Coping with Pet Loss.
www.veterinarywisdom.com/petparents, excellent resource for many
        aspects of pet care.

Commentary

Of life and death and love and dogs

I've lost my best buddy. But even now, perhaps he's showing me the way. August 2, 2015 — 10:14am

Down in the country, summer has passed its dazzling zenith — if only just.

Amid the farms and bluffs of southeastern Minnesota, where I've long been fortunate enough to squander occasional summer afternoons, the days on one recent late-July weekend still seemed lazy and lingering — but not quite so endless as they had felt only weeks before.

A few of the blazing perennial blossoms had begun to fade and wither. The sea of corn buffeted by the breeze all across the rolling hills — some of it immensely tall now — had lost its deepest jungle green and commenced the turn from growth to ripening.

It might just be me, of course, imposing this patina and pathos on an impassive landscape. I often am what people call "too serious." And lately I have an excuse.

My closest companion, best buddy and spiritual adviser has died. He was a 12-year-old collie mix, a courageous and mischievous goofball named Lucky who taught me the kind of things only the four-legged angels who visit our world can teach. I recognize the shameless self-indulgence involved in bothering readers with my grief over a lost pet. There's nothing very special, much less newsworthy, about the experience. But maybe that's the point.

Life delivers more fearful and devastating blows than the loss of a beloved animal, but many have shared (or will share) this startlingly bone-deep pain and lonesomeness. By confessing it, maybe I can hope in some small way to help us all comfort one another.

My fellow hobby farmer, Cindy, found Lucky as a stray puppy down in the country 12 years ago this summer. I theatrically proclaimed him "a gift to us" and lobbied against her reservations to turn the rescue into an adoption. It worked, and before long it became perfectly clear that Lucky loved Cindy best.

For eight playful, uproarious years, Lucky chased balls and Frisbees and swam after sticks thrown in the lake, romped with canine buddies, embarked on occasional unauthorized neighborhood "rounds," and delighted in games of keep-away and tug-of-war, especially just before bedtime. Then, four years ago, he went suddenly blind.

Life was sadly diminished after that, but Lucky soldiered on. And we, truth be told, followed his lead. He suffered many stumbles, was bruised by many obstacles, but he found his way to the joys that could still be reached, rather as he found his way up and down stairs — lifting a paw into the air and sticking it out into the darkness, feeling for the next step.

William James, the great early-20th-¬century philosopher and psychologist, once wrote an essay about what he called our "vital secrets" — the often hidden feelings that make lives worth living by "giving to foolishness a place ahead of power."

James lamented that modern people "are trained to seek the choice, the rare, the exquisite, and to overlook the common ... the peculiar sources of joy connected with our simpler functions."

"To be imprisoned or shipwrecked," he added, "would permanently show the good of life to many an overeducated pessimist."

We pass half-conscious, James wrote, through lives "replete with too much luxury, or tired and careworn about personal affairs." We rarely recognize "the indisputable fact that this world never did anywhere or at any time contain more of essential divinity, or of eternal meaning, than is embodied in the fields of vision over which (our) eyes so carelessly pass."

"There is life; and there, a step away, is death. There is the only kind of beauty there ever was."

Every dog, not just Lucky, has a genius for giving foolishness a place ahead of power. That's why befriending them is so enlightening for overeducated pessimists, and somewhat less taxing than prison or shipwreck.

Lucky had a quirk that taught me something else.

He hated going to the vet — really hated it. From puppyhood, even every routine check-up was a trauma. We got through them, and of course he always forgave me for what to him seemed bizarre lapses into sadism on my part.

So here was a creature experiencing something that seemed to him purely horrible — and without any possible purpose that he could conceive.

And yet, I knew, from a slightly different perspective, that these waking nightmares befell him entirely for his own good — and only because he was loved.

I've long liked to think of that as a metaphor for our own dark days. Maybe, from a slightly different perspective, there is a kindly purpose for things that aren't easy to understand.

That thought, anyway, helps me to follow Lucky's example, sticking a foot out into the darkness in hopes of finding the next step.

D.J. Tice is at Doug.Tice@startribune.com.

Peaceful Passing *for* Pets®

Scope of Our Offering

IMMEDIATE HELP

Initial phone consultation to:

- Identify need for veterinarian referral
- Explain services/options for care
- Describe role of Care Coordinator
- Schedule a Care Coordinator visit
- Provide resources on pet hospice care

MULTIDISCIPLINARY TEAM

- Referring Veterinarian
- Hospice Veterinarian
- Hospice Care Coordinator
- Social Worker
- Chaplain
- Vet Technician
- Complementary Veterinary Therapists

Pet & Pet Family

CARE COORDINATOR

- Expert in:
  - Hospice philosophy of care
  - Grief and loss
  - Human-Animal bond
- Serves as extension of referring veterinarian
- Creates a Plan of Care with veterinarian & pet family

PET FAMILY RESOURCES

- Peacefulpassingforpets.org
- 'A Caregiver's Guide to Pet Hospice Care'
- Pet Memorial Options
- Professional grief support

Building our foundation in Minnesota with anticipation our program will be replicated in other states.
www.peacefulpassingforpets.org

Canine Brief Pain Inventory

Description of pain:
Rate your dog's pain:

1. Fill in the oval next to the one number that best describes the pain at its **worst** in the last 7days.

◯0   ◯1   ◯2   ◯3   ◯4   ◯5   ◯6   ◯ 7   ◯ 8   ◯ 9   ◯ 10

No pain   Extreme pain

2. Fill in the oval next to the one number that best describes the pain at its **least** in the last 7 days

◯0   ◯1   ◯2   ◯3   ◯4   ◯5   ◯6   ◯ 7   ◯ 8   ◯ 9   ◯ 10

No pain   Extreme pain

3. Fill in the oval next to the one number that best describes the pain at its **average** in the last 7 days.

◯0   ◯1   ◯2   ◯3   ◯4   ◯5   ◯6   ◯ 7   ◯ 8   ◯ 9   ◯ 10

No pain   Extreme pain

4. Fill in the oval next to the one number that best describes the pain as it is **right now**.

◯0   ◯1   ◯2   ◯3   ◯4   ◯5   ◯6   ◯ 7   ◯ 8   ◯ 9   ◯ 10

No pain   Extreme pain

Description of function:

Fill in the oval next to the one number that best describes how during the last 7 days **pain has interfered** with your dog's:

5. General Activity

◯0   ◯1   ◯2   ◯3   ◯4   ◯5   ◯6   ◯ 7   ◯ 8   ◯ 9   ◯ 10

Does not interfere   Completely interferes

6. Enjoyment of Life

◯0   ◯1   ◯2   ◯3   ◯4   ◯5   ◯6   ◯ 7   ◯ 8   ◯ 9   ◯ 10

Does not interfere   Completely interferes

7. Ability to Rise to Standing From Lying Down

◯0   ◯1   ◯2   ◯3   ◯4   ◯5   ◯6   ◯ 7   ◯ 8   ◯ 9   ◯ 10

Does not interfere   Completely interferes

Brief Pain Inventory, con't

8. **Ability to Walk**

○0 ○1 ○2 ○3 ○4 ○5 ○6 ○ 7 ○ 8 ○ 9 ○ 10
Does not interfere   Completely interferes

9. **Ability to Run**

○0 ○1 ○2 ○3 ○4 ○5 ○6 ○ 7 ○ 8 ○ 9 ○ 10
Does not interfere   Completely interferes

10. **Ability to Climb Stairs, Curbs, Doorsteps, etc.**

○0 ○1 ○2 ○3 ○4 ○5 ○6 ○ 7 ○ 8 ○ 9 ○ 10
Does not interfere   Completely interferes

Overall impression:

11. Fill in the oval next to the one number that best describes your dog's overall quality of life over the last 7 days.

○ Poor   ○ Fair   ○ Good   ○ Very Good   ○ Excellent

MEDICATION FLOWSHEET

Patient Name

Allergies

DATE		MEDICATION	WHAT IS IT FOR?	DATE	WHEN DO I GIVE IT?				
Start	Stop	Dosage/Direction/Amount		Month & Day	Morning	Noon	Evening	Bedtime	Other

Note: Place an "X" in the box under time of day medication is to be taken.

Appendix

MEDICATION FLOWSHEET

Patient Name

Allergies

DATE	MEDICATION	WHAT IS IT FOR?	DATE	WHEN DO I GIVE IT?				
Start / Stop	Dosage/Direction/Amount		Month & Day	Morning	Noon	Evening	Bedtime	Other

Note: Place an "X" in the box under time of day medication is to be taken.

73

MEDICATION FLOWSHEET

Patient Name

Allergies

DATE Start / Stop	MEDICATION Dosage/Direction/Amount	WHAT IS IT FOR?	DATE Month & Day	WHEN DO I GIVE IT?				
				Morning	Noon	Evening	Bedtime	Other

Note: Place an "X" in the box under time of day medication is to be taken.

J - O - U - R - N - E - Y - S
A Quality of Life Scale for Pets
Dr. Katie Hilst, DVM

 I developed this Quality of Life Scale after hundreds of conversations over the years with pet owners and their families making the decision to euthanize their pet.

Sometimes, after the discussion, people realize that their pet is enjoying life, and they still have time left with their pet. Other times, people realize their pets are suffering more than they were aware, so they choose the final act of caring.

In either case, the JOURNEYS scale is meant to get you thinking and considering the factors that affect your pet's happiness and sense of well-being. There are no hard and fast rules, although in general a higher score is better. A score of 80 is a happy, healthy pet! A score of 8 is a pet that is suffering. A low score on any of the measures may be a reason to consider euthanasia. Please use this as a starting place to explore your pet's quality of life, and address your concerns with your veterinarian. I am available to discuss your pet too.

JOURNEYS :

J - Jumping or Mobility

O - Ouch or Pain

U - Uncertainty and Understanding (factors that affect YOU)

R - Respiration or Breathing

N - Neatness or Hygiene

E - Eating and Drinking

Y - You

S - Social Ability

For each variable there is an assigned value of 10 points with an example for scores of 1, 5 and 10 as guidance. Use your judgment to decide how your pet scores. **Example: E - Eating and Drinking**, if your pet "only eats treats" you may assign a value of 2 or 3- higher than 1 which is not eating at all, but less than 5 which is eating slightly less of their regular food than is normal for them.

J- Jumping or mobility:

1pt: Your pet cannot walk or stand without assistance.

5pt: Your pet can move around as long as he/she has their pain medication. They can do about half the activities they did when they were healthier, or can get about half the distance on a walk, or spend half the time doing their activities (chasing a Frisbee, swimming, hunting) as they used to.

10pt: Your pet is fully active and enjoying all their activities.

web: <u>JourneysPet</u>   JOURNEYS A Quality of Life Scale for Pets

O - Ouch or pain:

1pt: Your pet seems painful (whining, crying, not willing to move) even while taking pain medication. Note: many animals will hide pain or weakness as a survival trait.

5pt: Your pet is on pain medications and they are helping at least 75% of the time.

10pt: Your pet is pain free.

U - Uncertainty and Understanding:

1pt: Your pet has a diagnosis (medical condition) that cannot be predicted. You may not understand the diagnosis, or the problem may be prone to sudden, catastrophic events.

5pt: Your pet has a medical condition that can change over time, is currently stable, and you are able to monitor it (with the help of your veterinarian) and make adjustments when necessary. You understand what to watch for, the treatment plan, and when your pet needs medical attention.

10pt: Your pet is happy and healthy; there are no medical issues beyond routine preventative care.

R - Respiration or breathing:

1pt: Your pet has severe episodes of difficulty breathing, coughing or open mouth breathing. They are not eating or drinking in an effort to breathe. At this point you should seek immediate medical attention for your pet.

5pt: Your pet has occasional bouts of coughing, wheezing, or exercise intolerance. They are short (less than 2 minutes) and they are on medication from your veterinarian that can be adjusted to help.

10pt: Your pet has no coughing, wheezing, or exercise intolerance.

N - Neatness or hygiene:

1pt: Your pet spends time laying in their urine and/or feces. They may be unable to control their elimination, or be unable to move after elimination. Your pet may have an external tumor or mass that is bleeding, foul smelling, and infected, and you are unable to keep it clean and/or bandaged. Your pet may have pressure sores (bed sores) from lying down and being unable to move.

5pt: Your pet may need assistance to urinate/defecate but they do not spend time lying in their waste. They are able to hold their urine/feces until they get assistance. They may have an external tumor or mass, but it can be kept clean and/or bandaged and it is not infected. They groom themselves, but may need assistance in some areas (example-rear end).

10pt: Your pet can urinate, defecate, and groom themselves without assistance. They have no medical issues that are causing them to have a bad odor. You can provide any care issues to address their hygiene (baths, trip to the groomer, anal gland expression, teeth cleaning, etc.)

E - Eating and drinking:

1pt: Your pet is refusing food and water. They may be vomiting or having diarrhea (or both). They may be nauseous. Cats may "hang out" at the water bowl, next to it, or with their heads hanging over it.

5pt: Your pet is eating more slowly, and is not as interested in food as they used to be. They may go back several times before they finish a meal. They are eating slightly less than usual, but are eating their regular food.

10pt: Your pet is eating and drinking normally.

Y - You:

1pt: You are constantly worried about your pet. You may not understand what is happening to them. You feel overwhelmed and stressed trying to provide for their needs. You may feel you are unable to provide for their needs physically, emotionally, or financially. You may be worried about how they will fare when you are away on an upcoming trip. There may be tension in the family and disagreement on how to proceed.

5pt: You understand your pet's condition, and are able, with some effort, to meet their needs. You may have concerns, but they are manageable.

10pt: You are easily able to meet your pet's needs, and not worried about any aspect of their care.

S - Social ability:

1pt: Your pet does not spend time with the family. They may hide, become irritable or snippy if bothered. Some pets that do not enjoy being petted may not seem to care if they are petted. Perhaps your pet is unable physically to get to the room where they usually spend time with others.

5pt: Your pet spends at least half the time with the family. They are not irritable or snippy. They happily greet you when you come home.

10pt: Your pet enjoys you, the family, and others (including other animals they may know), greets you at the door when you arrive home, and seeks out company.

Dr. Katie Hilst is caring and compassionate, dedicated to making your pets last moments comfortable and peaceful. She is a proud graduate of the UW Veterinary School. Dr. Katie has been providing in home euthanasia in the Madison area longer than any other in-home euthanasia veterinarian. She offers in home euthanasia in the Madison Wisconsin and surrounding areas. She has over 10 years of veterinary experience, the past 5 years dedicated exclusively to home visits. ("It's My Calling").

She established Journeys Home to focus her efforts on helping pets and their families at the end of their lives She authored the JOURNEYS quality of life scale for pets in 2013, and is certified in Pet Loss and Grief Companioning.

Please visit on the web journeyspet.com . Phone consultations welcome. Call (608) 347-1897

(This document may be reproduced with links to the website and credit to the author intact.)

A

B

bereavement support, 2
bladder and bowel problems, 17–19
blogs (mnpets.com), 7
bowel and bladder problems, 17–19

C

CARE, 2, 11
Care Coordinator, 11, 15
care plan, 11
cats, giving medications to, 35–36
Certified Veterinary Spinal Manipulative Therapist (CVSMT), 26
children, bereavement, 58–60
chiropractic treatment, 26
Clough, Dr. Eric, 4–5
Clough, Jane, 4–5
Colorado State University Veterinary Teaching Hospital (www.
  argusinstitute.colostate.edu, Colorado State University Veterinary
  Teaching Hospital, 29
Colorado State Veterinary Teaching Hospital (csu-cvmbs.colostate.
  edu/, Search: Pet Hospice), 53
Colorado State Veterinary Teaching Hospital (csu-cvmbs.colostate.
  edu/vth/diagnostic-and-support/argus/pet-hospice, Colorado State
  University Veterinary Teaching Hospital), 12
COMFORT treatment, 2, 11
Coping With Sorrow, on the loss of your pet, 53
costs of end-of-life care, 10
Cremation Services (www.petsrememberedcremation.com), 53
CVSMT. *See* Certified Veterinary Spinal Manipulative Therapist
  (CVSMT)

D

detecting pain, 21–22
diapers, 18
diarrhea, 17–19
A Dog Years, 43
A Dog Years: A Memoir, 45
Doty, Mark, 45
dying, care for, 1–2

E

ear medications, giving, 38
Elizabethan (lampshade) collars, 38
end of life, decisions for. *See* euthanasia
equipment resources, 19
euthanasia
    before and after, 50-51
    burials and memorials, 51–52
    deciding the time, 43–47
    at home, 6–7
    introduction to, 41–43
    question of guilt, 47–49
eye medications, giving, 36–38

F

Facing Farewell: Making the Decision to Euthanize Your Pet, 46
Facing Farewell, Making the Decision to Euthanize Your Pet, 53
family members, emotional needs, 10
food and sick pet, 15–17

G

Goldberg, Katherine (DVM), 6

H

Hancock, Guy (DVM), 6
Help 'Em Up Dog Harness (helpemup.com), 19
Henson, Michael (DVM), 42
Hilst, Katie (DVM), 44
holistic care, 4
In Home Euthanasia National Directory
  (inhomepeteuthanasia.com), 53
Home VET Hospice, 6
hospice, defined, 1
hospice care, vi–vii
    humans, history of, 1–3
    veterinary hospice for pets, 4–7
How Animals Grieve, 62
hydration and nutrition, 15–17

I

IAAHPC. *See* International Association of Animal Hospice and Palliative Care (IAAHPC)
Iams Pet Loss Support Hotline, (1-888-332-7738), 62
www.iccfa.comnode/2562/AboutPLPA, 53
If It Should Be, 41
injections, giving, 39
International Association of Animal Hospice and Palliative Care (IAAHPC), 5–7
International Veterinary Acupuncture Society (www.ivas.org), 29

K

Kaplan, Laurie, 53
Katz, Jon, 45
King, Barbara, 63

L

laser therapy, 27
Of life and death and love and dogs, 55–56, 64–68
lift carriers, jackets and harnesses, 14–15
lifting adaptations, 14–15
liquid medications, giving, 34–35

M

Magic Dog, 57
Marrachino, Kathy (Ph.D.), 5
massage, 28–29
McComas, Rebecca (DVM), 53
medications, giving
    administering liquid medications, 34–35
    administering pills, 33–34
    cautions for, 31–32
    giving ear medications to cats or dogs, 38
    giving eye medications to cats or dogs, 36–38
    giving injections, 39
    giving medications by mouth to cats, 35–36
    giving skin medications to cat or dog, 38
Mernit, Judith Lewis, 62
MN Pets, gentle end of life care at home (mnpets.com), 12

N

National Board of Certification for Animal Acupressure & Massage (www.nbcaam.org), 29
National Pet Owners Survey, 2011-2012, 4
Nikki Hospice Foundation, 5
nutrition and hydration, 15–17

O

oral medications, 23–25

P

pain control
    acupuncture, 25–26
    chiropractic treatment, 26
    detecting pain, 22–23
    laser therapy, 27
    oral medications, 23–25
    other therapies, 27–28
    "Pepper," story of, 21–22
palliative care, 3
Pawspice, CA, 43, 48
Peaceful Passing for Pets®, MN (peacefulpassingforpets.org), vii, 7, 12, 19, 29, 62, 72–76
"Pepper," story of, 21–22
pet bed, adaptations, 13–15
pet hospice
    decisions for, 9–11
    team members available to clients, 11
Pet Loss and Bereavement (www.sayinggoodbyetoyourangelanimals.com), 53
Pet Loss Professional Alliance (www.iccfa.comnode/2562/AboutPLPA), 53
Pet Loss Support page (www.pet-loss.net), 53
pet owners and terminally ill pets, v
Pet Quality of Life Scale and Daily Diary (www.lapoflove.com), 53
pets, as family members, 4–5
pets, bereavement, 61–62

V

W

Y

ADVANCE PRAISE

"This is an informative book that covers all aspects of what veterinary hospice means, including the physical, emotional, and psychological needs of the pet owner and their pet. It is a valuable resource for those who are dealing with end of life choices for their beloved companion."

– Ann Fischer, DVM

"We love them so much, we want tender loving care for our pets through all stages of life, including near the end. Having choices in care is empowering and provides the best opportunity for comfort, dignity, and peace for all members of the family, two-legged and otherwise. Palliative care and hospice are the right choices for many families when their pets become ill. This long-awaited resource provides much needed help for the caregivers and, through them, the pets they love."

– Michael Henson DVM, PhD, DACVIM

"Is there anything that could give any of us more peace then to know that we helped our faithful friend pass from this life with the utmost love and care?"

– Rebecca McComas, DVM

"Grateful. Wow. This is a real gift to those of us who are loving and supporting our beloved furry family members through the last part of their lives. As a Chaplain, I hear many peoples stories about struggling alone with questions and fears. This amazing resource brings hope and help and comfort. It's accessible and full of heart."

– The Rev. Mary Piper, Chaplain

Notes